The Buyers Magnet: How to Craft So Appealing Offers That No One Would Resist

Bernie D. Martino

TABLE OF CONTENT

INTRODUCTION

Every organization needs to stand out as the beacon of success in the business sector since customer/client loyalty and competitiveness have never been higher. In order to succeed as a business owner, you must constantly be looking for new customers/clients. Even if you have a core group of devoted customers, growing your business over time requires encouraging them to return and luring in new clients.

Make sure that your business is always friendly to potential clients and customers. You can continue to provide exceptional customer service and innovate your business and products, thanks to the influx of various clientele. New customers keep you on your toes and provide the business with new revenue streams. It's time to think of some fresh, original ways to market your company and entice customers/clients to buy your goods if sales are starting to slow down or become stagnant.

"The Buyer's Magnet" is more than simply a book; it's a revolutionary credo for business owners, salespeople, and executives alike. Whether you're a startup trying to make a name for yourself or an established business trying to resurrect your brand, this book will provide you with ideas and strategies to create offers that are so irresistible that no one will be able to refuse them.

In chapter one of this book, because the author understands that the revenue and profitability of a firm can be significantly impacted by its pricing strategy, you will be learning different pricing strategies and pricing techniques that will put your business ahead of your competitors. In contrast to a badly designed pricing strategy, which can result in fewer profits and decreased revenue, a successful adoption of a good pricing strategy can increase your results by between 10% and 30%. This chapter does not end there, it went ahead to unveil how to find the proper market and how to get people buying your product.

Having learnt all the pricing strategies, the right market and how to get them buyers, the question now is what are you offering in exchange for the price? How valuable is it? Is it worth the price? Chapter 2 has the answers to these questions as the author is going to be holding your hands and walking you through the importance of creating values and offers, how to create these offers, the challenges, solutions and how to build a strong reputation to stand out among many competitors. The chapter 3, being the last chapter of interesting and incredible book is design to teach you how you can enhance this offers you have created to keep people glued to you while always looking forward to what you have next as they wouldn't want to miss any chance of buying and benefiting from the wealth of values that come with your product.

CHAPTER 1

1.1 PRICING

The price of your goods or service is one of the most important business decisions you'll make. Setting a pricing that is either too high or too low may, at best, prevent your business from growing. Your sales and cash flow could, at worst, be adversely impacted.

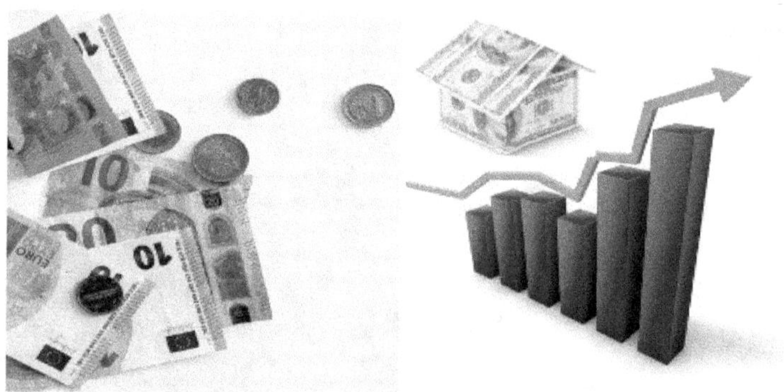

1.1.1 Product Pricing Strategy

A product pricing strategy is a way to price your products with the goal of figuring out the price that makes the most profit and that is located in the "sweet spot," where pricing isn't deemed neither too high to lose sales nor too low to negatively affect your margins. There are four methods for pricing products, you must choose the type of pricing strategy you want to use when pricing products. Your chosen strategy will rely on your goods and your rivals. These are the four most widely used pricing strategies:

1. Expensive Prices

Most people are fairly knowledgeable about what is affordable and what is pricey. Your product must feel pricey if you plan to charge a high price. It's your responsibility to raise its perceived value.

Attempt this exercise: Consider a couple luxury and a few budget brands. List each one's traits in writing. What distinguishes them? What distinguishes premium brands from budget ones?

Take hotels for example, many hotels offer opulent rooms, beautiful dining, gorgeous décor, and top-notch amenities, but what distinguishes a five-star hotel from the competition is that they are able to anticipate their guests' needs and their staff and management's unwavering commitment to providing exceptional, personalized service each and every time.

In order to be given the five-star designation, you must provide lavished accommodation with lots of amenities and everyone knows that five star hotels are quite pricey compared to others.

Factors that increase a product's perceived value include:

- **Design and packaging** Every expensive thing you purchase is packaged elegantly. Your item ought to "look" pricey. This is also possible with digital goods. Simply spend some time on visiting websites for high-end products and pay attention to what makes those websites appear pricey. Make your website appear pricey to start, and then make your goods appear upscale as well. PDFs and ebooks will always seem inexpensive when it comes to information items. Everyone is aware of how easy and inexpensive it is to create a PDF. We advise opposing it. Information items delivered on tangible media, online courses, and e-learning settings will always seem more valuable. For instance, if the competition is selling ebooks on your subject, create a video offering. Products using video always appear more refined than those with text-only.

- **Uniqueness:** Expensive goods must be unique and the only ones available that perform the desired function. You truly can't charge more than the market average if your goods in a crowded market lacks any distinguishing qualities (unless you artificially create that uniqueness with something like a brand-owned word).

- **Availability:** If you have a very small number of individuals (for instance, a coaching program that only accepts 25 participants), you can charge a higher price. If you can satisfy all four of the aforementioned criteria, going with a high pricing plan can be quite beneficial. Things to keep in mind with pricey good.

- One of three pricing techniques that can boost earnings is this one. (The other two are selling more things or selling to more people.)

People immediately believe a product is better when it costs more money. Example: Last month, I purchased two vehicles. The first one was $10,000, and the second one was $85,000. What automobile is superior? To respond to the question, you don't need to know anything else.

Desire = different + pricey.

Once you've established that your product is pricey, every time you make a sale, your income will increase dramatically. (However, avoid doing it too frequently to avoid upsetting the clients who paid the higher price.)

2. Low cost pricing

You will always compete on price if your product is not distinctive. People will choose based on pricing if there are no discernible distinctions between your goods and that of your competitors. That could be advantageous for you.

Being less expensive is the best pricing approach in a cutthroat market. (Warren Buffett claims that Geico's economic moat is exactly that.) People prefer to buy things on sale. If your product is quite comparable to others on the market, this is the ideal course of action.

It's not necessary to be the cheapest in order to have low product prices. It's a good idea to experiment with your product's price being greater than normal. You quickly improve your profits if you test a higher price and it receives the same volume of answers as the lower price.

A greater price will typically result in fewer sales. According to the principle of market elasticity, sales would decline as prices rise and vice versa.

As the price rises, a product with elastic demand will sell fewer units. (Source of image)

The current issue is how much. You will do better with increased pricing if there is only a modest decline because you will generate more money (and potentially draw in higher-quality clients who will spend more money in the future).

Because there will not be enough new customers coming in, if you set the price too high, your sales will plummet and you will not be able to maintain cash flow. Usually, this is easy to see and fix.

When you join a market with a product that is not significantly better than that of your rivals, you usually win by providing a discount.

When there is a predetermined price for the same kind of product, the buyer may more quickly calculate the average price. You might attract a lot of interest if you can sell at a significant discount.

You must decide if you can afford to run your business in that way.

3. Niche product pricing

So exactly does being a "nobody" relate to pricing? So it stands to reason that if you do not have a big name, you can not expect a high price.

The truth is that even if website visitors have no idea who you are, you could still be able to sell your goods for a fair price. No matter how big or little your offering is (for instance, a single video vs. a series of films), you can still be successful.

The following are the stages to implement a niche product pricing strategy:
As many related products to your niche as you can list their prices for. I use the term

"comparable" to describe products with the same market and customer base.

Please list the top three products. You believe that these products pose the biggest risk to your potential client.

Consider the following: Are you the only one with your goods and it is a fresh offering? If the product is intended for customers, charge 20–50% more than the most expensive alternative (if there is one). If it is intended for business people, charge 30–100% more than the most expensive things. Does your product provide a current benefit that is distinct from that of your competitors'? Decide on a price that lies halfway between the lowest and highest goods. Are you providing the same product in a different format (for example, a video instead of print)? Choose a cost that is halfway between the item's lowest and highest prices.

Different demographics are represented among online customers. Some individuals think that the word "free" denotes mediocrity or inferior quality. Because they feel they have been taken advantage of by offers of free things, they may be distrustful of them. Similar to when a product is overpriced, some purchasers could feel suspicious. Costly goods are frequently linked to great quality.

The defense I frequently hear, at least from info product makers, is that if you price low, you make up for it in volume. Not at all. Most people grossly underestimate the number of possible consumers of their product. If you had predicted 1,000, you may have predicted 500. The difference between selling for $9.95 and $22.95 will have a big impact on your bottom line.

4. The ideal pricing strategy

Before settling on your price, you must have some idea of how much space you have. A wise place to start is by getting a clear picture of your costs. Fixed costs and variable costs are two categories of costs.

Variable costs are those costs you incur that are directly tied to the products you offer. For instance, if you sold a Blu-ray instructional video course on "How to grow healthy houseplants," your variable cost-per-item would comprise the price of the Blu-ray discs, any rights fees you might have to pay for each film sold, and the cost of delivery.

Your variable cost-per-product would need to rise by $10 for customer acquisition if you pay Google $0.20 per click and every 50th visitor converts to a customer.

Fixed costs are the costs you incur to keep your firm running. These consist of the wages for your employees, the rent for the office, Internet costs, utility costs, and so forth.

The cost of your product has a huge effect on sales. Choosing a price is a rather straightforward process, much like choosing a medium or a commodity.

Start by observing what your competitors are doing. If your competitors are already charging that much for their widgets, think about charging $175 for yours. It is reasonable to believe that any product that has been selling well for $175 has been tried at numerous price points, both higher and lower, and that $175 is the price where the money is.

In order to be successful, you must select the pricing that will generate the highest profits from your selling campaign. Knowing the ideal pricing is essential because it can change over the course of a product's lifecycle (increasing, for instance, when it becomes popular). If you go too far from it, you will wind yourself losing money when you could have made it.

After you have considered your costs, the value of your product, and your position in the market, it is time to decide on a price.

Observe the following points:

- It is better to impose higher fees. Consumer perceptions of your product's quality increase with price. If your pricing is initially on the low side, as opposed to when your product is slightly overpriced, you will experience more resistance from your customers when you try to raise it.

- Don't limit your small business's competition to pricing wars. It's typically a better idea for a smaller e-commerce company to compete on additional value rather than pricing. Larger rivals with more resources and lower operating expenses crush you in a price war.

- Consider the American market and use American currency while selling to a global audience. The Internet uses the dollar as its official currency, without a doubt. The majority of online transactions use US currency.

- Prices are important. Never ask for $100 . Instead, charge $99.95! Don't charge more than $100; if you want to charge more, stop at $105. Select the following natural bracket, say $109.95.

- If it's feasible and your product is pricey, consider offering installment payments or financing. Since many people are strapped for cash, extending a special discount to them might greatly increase sales. Why do you think so many merchants advertise "Zero money down!" Offering customers the choice of financing or monthly payments can boost sales.

1.1.2 Advanced Pricing Techniques

The contrast principle

Perform this test at home. Three bowls should be filled with water: one with cold water, one with hot water, and one with lukewarm water. Your hands should be in the cold and hot water, respectively. Do not let them out for 30 seconds. Now submerge your hands in the warm water. Both hands are warm; one is chilly. The contrast principle is this.

Nothing is costly or affordable. It is what you measure it against. Putting $3,000 shoes next to $800 shoes is the best way to sell them. With pricey goods, this works fantastically. You can make them appear more affordable when compared to other goods.

Visit any upscale shopping location to observe how this is accomplished. Watch shops only stock $50,000 timepieces to make the $3,000 watch appear more affordable.

Decoy pricing

When a company uses decoy pricing, it offers clients a range of costs in an effort to sway them toward a specific product or service, also known as the target. The decoy, a slightly less enticing alternative, makes the target appear more alluring. This pricing approach takes use of our inclination psychologically to avoid products or services we judge to be of low quality or value.

To alter how consumers view the available options, a decoy pricing method is employed. Sellers rely on the decoy effect to persuade clients that the more expensive and profitable item is the best deal.

When to use decoy pricing

There are several ways to use decoy pricing that could increase sales for your company.

Variable pricing

Depending on a product's attributes or characteristics, it is priced at various levels, or tiers. By demonstrating that the top tier has more features in comparison to the cost, you can make it more appealing. You have three products, for instance:

Item A: $25, three attributes

item B: $40, four characteristics,

*item C: $45, seven features, fo*r

Product C provides three additional features than Product B for $5 extra. The ruse is Product B. Its purpose is to make Product C appear more valuable and deserving of its higher price.

Bundling

Combining your goal products with additional offerings that clients will find valuable, while framing the decoy as the less desirable choice. Consider that you sell bike equipment online. You market goods as follows:

- Nameless gym pants: $40
- Branded gym pants: $75
- Package deal: branded gym pants and gloves: $85

The gloves usually cost $25. The branded clothing serves as a ruse. Due to the attraction effect, clients wind up spending more money overall on the expensive choice of the package deal.

1.1.3 Various pricing strategies

Using various strategies can increase your consumer base and boost your bottom line.

- **Discounting** Offering exceptional discounts can be a potent marketing strategy. This could be a sale price reduction to move outdated inventory, a discount for buying multiples of the same or related goods, or a discount for larger orders. By lowering expenses, you ought to be able to increase the profitability of these. But take care. Customers may doubt your full-rate pricing or view you as a cheap alternative if you discount excessively, making it challenging to charge full-rate prices in the future.

- **Odd value pricing** If pricing is a key factor in customers' purchasing decisions, then the retailer's strategy of selling things for \$9.99 instead of \$10 can be helpful. Customers sometimes find strange value prices like this to be more alluring.

- **Loss leader** Selling a product for a low or even loss-making price falls under this category. Even while you might lose money on this product, it might draw clients who will buy other, more lucrative products.

- **Skimming** You might command a premium price for a special good or service. Skimming is what this is known as, but you must be certain that what you are selling is distinctive. If there is real competition, you might simply price yourself out of the market.

- **Penetration** Starting at a low price and capturing market share before rivals catch up to you is the opposite of skimming.

You should be able to find ways to increase costs later if you have a base of devoted customers.

- **Raising or lowering prices** You'll occasionally need to adjust your prices. But before you do, you should evaluate how any suggested pricing change would affect your profitability.

1.1.4 Pricing Growth

Even if your sales volume may decline, raising pricing can increase your profitability.

Always provide your consumers an explanation if you are raising your prices. You might take advantage of the pricing change to reiterate the advantages you have to offer. Additionally, a thorough justification might improve your rapport with a client.

Additionally, there are methods for concealing price rises. You could, for instance:

Reduce the specification and your costs while retaining the same price by introducing new, more expensive goods or services and rendering previous, less expensive ones obsolete.

However, be cautious that if your customers find out what you're doing, they can react negatively.

lowering costs

Never make a price reduction choice impulsively. Is this the image you want to project for your business? Low costs frequently go hand in hand with subpar service.

Instead of lowering prices to increase sales, focus on increasing profits. Most of the time, your clients choose to purchase from you due to the advantages you provide as well as your price.

Rarely is a decision taken exclusively on the basis of cost

1.2 HOW TO FIND THE PROPER MARKET AMONGST A FAMISHED POPULACE

Identifying your target audience

Knowing your target market is crucial before you launch a firm. This will enable you to concentrate your marketing efforts and make sure the proper audiences are being reached.

Your target market might be outlined in a number of different ways. The first step is to consider the characteristics of your potential client. Age, gender, geography, and income are a few examples of these variables.

Consider what your target market needs or wants from your product or service once you have a general sense of who they are. What are the aches and pains? What are they aiming for?

Consider your target market in terms of psychographics as well. This comprises elements like way of life, principles, and attitudes.

You may start developing marketing initiatives aimed at reaching your target market once you have a solid understanding of it. Targeted advertisements, social media posts, and email marketing are a few examples of this.

Your target market may evolve over time, so keep that in mind. You might discover that as your company expands, you need to modify your marketing initiatives to attract new clients.

Researching your target market

It's crucial to spend time researching your target market before you begin marketing your goods or services. This will assist you in deciding how to effectively reach your target clients and where to concentrate your marketing efforts.

There are several methods for researching your target market. Start by examining demographic information such as age, gender, locality, and income level. You can use this to acquire a general idea of the characteristics and potential needs of your target market.

Examining your target market's purchasing patterns is another technique to conduct market research. What they purchase, and why? How frequently do they buy things? What drives their purchasing choices? You may use this knowledge to develop a marketing plan that appeals to their wants and requirements.

Finally, you may employ focus groups and surveys to obtain opinions about your goods and services from potential clients. This can be a priceless way to discover what people like and dislike as well as the qualities they seek in a good or service.

You'll be able to develop a marketing strategy that targets your precise target market once you've done your study. This will enable you to make the most of your marketing money and guarantee that your message reaches the intended audience.

Analyzing your target market

It's critical to consider the target market while developing a product or service. To make sure that your product or service satisfies the needs of your target market, a procedure known as market analysis is used.

There are several ways to go about conducting a market analysis. The first step is to assess your target market's needs and determine how your product or service will satisfy them. This entails first determining the demands and desires of your target market before developing a product or service to fulfill those desires.

Examining the opposition is the second strategy. This entails doing research to find out what alternative goods or services are offered that satisfy the requirements of your target market. You can conduct this research online, through trade journals, or by speaking with individuals in your target market. You may develop a good product or service that outperforms what is already on the market if you have a solid understanding of the competition.

Combining the first two strategies is the third technique. This implies that you evaluate both your target market's and the competition's needs before developing a good or service that more effectively satisfies your target market. This strategy is frequently the most successful since it enables you to develop a good or service that is truly distinctive.

After conducting a market analysis, you should have a clear understanding of your target market's characteristics and needs. From there, you can begin to develop a good or service that satisfies their requirements.

Identifying your target market's needs

It's critical to initially determine the needs of your target market if you have a product or service you wish to promote. This will assist you in deciding how to position your product and the kind of marketing that will appeal to potential clients.

There are several approaches to this. You might start by investigating the demographics of your target market. Age, gender, income, geography, and degree of education are a few examples of these. Psychographics, which are elements that characterize a person's personality, values, and lifestyle, are another option.

Once you have a firm grasp of your target market's demographic and psychographic traits, you can start to think about their wants. What characteristics do they look for in a comparable good or service to yours? What might make their life better or easier?

Some requirements are practical, such as the desire for an item that is less expensive or simpler to use. Others are emotional, such as the desire for a product to boost one's self-esteem or physical attractiveness. And still some are social, such as the demand for a product that fosters social interaction.

You can begin to build a marketing strategy that will appeal to your target market once you have a firm grasp of their demands. The development of new product features that meet particular demands, the creation of content that speaks to the needs of your target market, or the development of focused advertising campaigns are some examples of how to do this.

Your marketing efforts are more likely to be successful if you take the time to comprehend the needs of your target market.

5. Developing a marketing mix

It's crucial to have a solid understanding of your target market before you begin marketing your goods or services. This will assist you in creating a marketing mix that appeals to your target market and encourages conversions.

There are a few important considerations to make when choosing your target market. To start, you must identify your ideal client. What characteristics do they have? What do they enjoy and disapprove of? What do they require and desire? You may start creating a marketing mix that will appeal to your target customer once you have a firm grasp of who they are.

The four Ps make up the marketing mix: product, pricing, location, and promotion. It's crucial to keep your target market in mind while choosing your marketing mix. The demands and desires of your target market should be satisfied by your product or service. They should be willing to pay any price you ask for. Additionally, your target market should be considered while choosing your location and promotion.

You'll be well on your way to success if you take the time to create a marketing mix that appeals to your target demographic.

Be patient. It takes time to identify the perfect market for your goods or service. Do not give up if you do not get results straight away. Consistently test new marketing strategies, and adjust as needed. With patience and perseverance, you will eventually find the best market for your business.

Evaluating your marketing efforts

You've at last produced a top-notch goods or service. You've put in many hours perfecting it, and you're sure it stands a good chance of making it big in the market. However, before you begin selling, you must be certain that the market you are aiming for is the proper one.

Evaluation of your previous marketing initiatives is the first step. Are the proper people receiving your message? Are you reaching your target market through the most efficient means possible? The most crucial question is: Are you receiving the outcomes you want?

If you're not satisfied with your marketing efforts, it's time to examine your target market more carefully. Start by posing these crucial queries to yourself:

- Who Is My Target Market, First?
- Which needs in my target market can my product or service meet?
- What Are My Target Market's Buying Patterns?
- What Are My Target Market's Demographics?

- How Do I Locate My Target Market?

You'll have a much better sense of who you should be directing your marketing efforts at once you've responded to these queries. From there, you can start to create a marketing strategy that is more specifically targeted and more likely to yield the desired outcomes.

Changing your marketing plan

You must first determine the appropriate market for your product or service if you want to properly advertise it. Understanding your target audience and their demands is the first step. You can change your marketing mix to appeal to them once you are aware of this.

The collection of components you use to sell your goods or service is known as the marketing mix. You can change any of these components to suit your target audience.

For instance, you might want to concentrate on social media promotion if you are marketing a product that is intended for a younger audience. You might want to concentrate on location and make sure your product is offered in the appropriate stores if you are marketing to a more older audience.

Finding the ideal mix of components that works for your product and your target market requires experimentation. Never be reluctant to experiment and change your marketing mix as you go. Finding the correct market for your good or service and making sure they are aware of it are the most crucial steps.

1.3 HOW TP GET CUSTOMERS TO BUY YOUR PRODUCT OR SERVICE

Describe how your products have benefited customers with real examples.

Additionally to providing product descriptions, it would be advantageous to list specific benefits. Make it clear to your audience how your products might satisfy their desire for ease or take care of their issues. To create instructive content and case studies of customers who have used your product successfully, hire a part-time virtual assistant.

Draw attention to the unique qualities of your products.

It is critical to set your brand out from the competitors. When selling your products to potential customers, emphasize the distinctive qualities of your offering. Additionally, customers will find it easier to remember your goods as a result.

Give somewhat more than is necessary.

Give your customers a little bit more. To improve your clients' opinion of you, include a bonus item or a reduced-size version of a new product in the packaging. A special offer like "buy now and get 10% off your next purchase" is another way to accomplish this. You can also establish a loyalty program to thank customers for their purchases.

This strategy might encourage customer loyalty.

Be accessible; make sure they can contact you right away if they have any questions.

Customers should be able to get in touch with you easily if they have questions regarding one of your products. Include a contact box on your website, and reply to feedback quickly on your social media pages. These will give your customers a voice and allow them to make suggestions. Getting their feedback will unquestionably help you improve your products and services and promote trust between your business and your customers.

There are many methods for convincing clients to buy your products, and they do not all have to entail pushy sales techniques.

CHAPTER 2.

2.1 IMPORTANCE OF CREATING VALUES AND OFFERS IN YOUR PRODUCTS

Do your potential customers recognize the worth of your offering? Have you taken all reasonable steps to improve the perceived worth of your goods or services? You create a positive experience for your clients and success for yourself when you make their needs your priority.

What is value perceived to be?

Customers are more likely to purchase from you if they believe that your product or service is worth their money. They get the warm, fuzzy sense that their choice is the right one.

According to Business Dictionary, perceived value refers to a customer's assessment of the worth of a product to that person. It may have little to nothing to do with the product's market pricing and instead depends on how well it can meet the customer's wants.

So how do you demonstrate to your prospective customer your product's ability to satisfy "his or her needs or requirements"?

1. **Increase room occupancy.** Pay attention to your customer's demand to buy rather than your own need to sell. Think about the advantages they will receive from your product or service. You achieve this by offering a remedy. The phrase "sell solutions/benefits and not features" refers to the idea that whatever you sell must address a specific issue. A solution is only provided when a client's problem is resolved by your product or service. This not only gives you a competitive edge, but it also strengthens your bond with your clients and enables you to prove your worth. By exceeding a customer's expectations, you can further prove your value. Discover their driving forces and go above and beyond what the opposition

is offering. In his story, Tom Reilly describes a driver who goes above and beyond by modifying his route to accommodate the needs of his passengers. "I want to make it simple for our customers to receive our deliveries," the man is heard stating in the recording. Others will not drive that way. This driver consistently gives his customers the result they desire since he is aware of what they want. He is improving their experience by doing this.

2. **Increase the perceived value with social proof:** Using social proof is another technique to raise the perceived worth of your service. Social proof can take many different forms, including client case

studies, client logos on your website, and testimonials. One common method of demonstrating social proof is through testimonials. A testimonial is a fantastic tool for streamlining the purchasing process. It adds context. By demonstrating to potential consumers that you have happy customers, you enhance conversion by demonstrating to them that you have happy customers as well. Even if your prospects believe you are prejudiced, they will still believe what your customers have to say. It is a good idea to add a picture of the individual providing the testimony when using testimonials. According to research, people enjoy looking at other people's faces. Therefore, if it is possible, attach a respectable photo to the testimonial. The "truthiness" of the claim is increased by adding a picture to the relevant testimonial since studies have shown that people are more likely to accept a claim as true when it is accompanied by a picture.

3. **Offer a contrast:** The contrast principle has been applied if you have ever contrasted one thing or person to another. When we compare someone to another, as when we say a woman is gorgeous or a man is handsome. The contrast principle can be used to a marketer's advantage. You contrast the product you want to sell with one of worse quality. Some marketers may display goods whose price range is far beyond what the intended customer can afford. This gives their goods a respectable appearance, which is

a method used to justify the quality and cost of their own goods or service. For instance, real estate brokers take advantage of the contrast tactic by showing prospective buyers a run-down or expensive home before the one they wish to sell. The realtor provides buyers with a benchmark against which to evaluate the home or property by doing this. The contrast principle can also be used to your advantage by offering a price comparison between your good or service and that of rival brands. Additionally, demonstrate to them how doing business with you will save them money.

4. Make your goods or service scarcer. One of the main reasons we purchase is scarcity. Additionally, you can raise the perceived worth of your service by introducing scarcity. A condition of scarcity occurs when there are few resources available and there is a high demand for those resources. Unique items are popular among people. something that is unique. Make your goods limited or available for a short period of time so that people will want it more. You might include a deadline when conducting a launch, for instance. The item is taken away once the deadline has passed. Alternatively, you may offer a discount with a deadline-based price increase. When the deadline arrives, some marketers offer bonuses that are no longer valid. Your actions are encouraging inactive prospects to take action. Humans naturally fear loss, therefore you make your prospects believe they would miss out if they do not take action right now. They will also feel dreadful.

5. **Keep the experience in mind:** Some marketers draw customers' attention by emphasizing money. However, emphasizing the experience a consumer has when using your product might result in their developing a lasting emotional bond with your company and its products.

2.2 HOW TO CREATE IRRESISTIBLE OFFERS

Existence of a strong and enticing proposition is the lifeblood of any company and the key to success in any activity. The better you are at creating the offer around whatever it is that you choose to sell, whether it be a good, service, or piece of knowledge, the more likely you are to be successful.

The problem? Most business owners struggle to identify the right target market and to develop their offer. But it is the offer that counts. Beyond your wildest dreams, it lays the way for explosive organizational growth while opening a door to untapped possibilities and income.

To make a convincing offer, you need to understand a few things at a fundamental level. You need to comprehend your customer completely. You also need to understand your specialization and the current business environment. Naturally, you must also be aware of your competitors. Your chances of creating an offer that the general public would find appealing will rise if you have a deeper understanding of these three criteria.

In total, there are seven elements that go into creating an alluring offer. They are all essential. If you are committed to making it in the business world, everyone of these must be present.

You are mainly squandering your time if you ignore even one of these seven principles, and you should not hope to succeed in any meaningful way.

As an alternative, if you adhere to these seven principles, you can anticipate success and gradual saturation of your offer. The framework is provided by the keys, but the key here is how you use them. You will be well on your way to market dominance if you take the time to comprehend and implement your offer correctly.

1. Be precise.

Being absolutely clear about what you are selling is the first step in building an enticing offer. People who are confused will not buy from you. Your copywriting talents will be necessary in this situation. If you want people to buy, make sure you create and provide a really clear and understandable offer.

The easiest approach to accomplish this is to clearly and concisely describe and communicate the goal of whatever it is that you are selling. Be precise in your response. Avoid using ambiguous language that does not accurately describe the offer. Make sure that the title is engaging, relevant to your audience, and makes a promise that can be kept by whatever it is you are selling. To illustrate the specifics of the offer, use numbers, dates, or percentages.

2. Present a superb value.

Value has become less prevalent in business. When it really needs to be the other way around, most people strive to labor as little as possible for the biggest reward. Whatever you are selling must offer enormous amounts of value. You might make some initial sales if you are just throwing something up and hoping to make a lot of money, but do not count on any consistency if your value is not high enough.

Offers that fall short of expectations will be mainly returned, challenged, and refuted. That headache should not be resting on your shoulders. You do not want negative or unfavorable press or reviews. Make a special effort to provide enormous amounts of value, and your offer will gain traction. Keep in mind that word of mouth spreads quickly. Additionally, unfavorable press can ruin your company for good.

3. Offer a reduction in price or a premium.

You need to convince clients to make an immediate purchase from you. You need to charge a premium or give a significant discount to accomplish it. What extras can you add to the deal to make it virtually impossible to refuse? Give this some serious thinking.

Keep in mind that the prospect has a very limited attention span. Without providing a premium service or a discount, you might not be able to readily override their objection if they have one. This is about making the deal enticing by adding extras rather than delivering extremely low prices.

4. Describe your proposal.

People are skeptics by nature. No matter who you are or what you are selling, people will need to be persuaded to take advantage of your offer. You need to give a very sound justification for your offer, regardless of whether you have developed a strong rapport with that person through time or not. What will it accomplish for the prospect? What will they be able to accomplish after they get it?

5. Demand a quick response.

Request a prompt response from your potential client. The scarcity principle must be taken into account in this case. The deal can expire in a few days or hours. Whatever it is that you are selling might only be available in very small quantities.

Whatever it is, you have to demand a response right away. convey the urgency of the situation. Because you might not see them again when they depart. Why do you think auto salespeople try to persuade you to make a quick purchase? They are aware that the prospects of locking in that sale drastically decrease once you leave.

6. Add a compelling call to action.

There needs to be a clear call to action in your offer. Inform the potential customer of your desired action. Consider them to be a 10-year-old who needs to be instructed on what to do next. You have probably seen this on the deals that are most alluring, where it instructs you on what to do next. For instance, click the green "buy now" button, fill out the form, and then download the item. or something comparable.

Use large, bold colors and buttons, and try to keep the website's clickable objects to a minimum. Remember that you want to guide the prospect in the proper direction while not overwhelming them with choices. For the same reason, offer pages should not have menus or other navigational elements.

7. Offer a bulletproof warranty.

If you want to sell on autopilot and have your offer succeed, give the prospect a steadfast guarantee that eliminates any risk. When the prospect thinks there is no danger involved, this will force them to act. This explains why almost every purchase comes with a 30-day money-back guarantee. The significance of making these guarantees is understood by astute marketers.

All you have to do is transfer the risk from the customer to yourself. This demonstrates your level of assurance that the buyer will adore whatever you have to give.

The significance of providing customers with value (rather than just items)

Customer value gauges how valuable a product is to a customer in comparison to potential competitors. Many firms use the following equation to calculate customer value: customer value = all benefits a customer obtains from a product, minus any challenges they face.

Some products provide practically no drawbacks and quick client value. For instance, if you just take a few seconds to fasten your seat belt in a car, it could save your life.

The improved customer value of a good or service often makes the challenge of obtaining or using it worthwhile. For instance, the consumer value of hot chocolate can make being in the chilly line acceptable. Similar to this, the cost of repairs may be higher for a premium vehicle.

8. You must differentiate yourself from rivals.
Most industries have at least a few rivals who all provide identical goods and services with similar pricing structures. You need to find strategies to set yourself apart from the competition if you want to stand out as a distinct company in your industry. Find strategies to differentiate your company from others that provide services to your industry.

Think about adding new products to ones that your rivals already sell. You might be able to extend the usefulness of your present items or reduce servicing fees for devoted customers.

Take action to consistently set yourself apart from the competition in the market. Consider offering a complementary pastry with each morning cup of coffee if your coffee shop is one of many on a popular street. You might provide free internet access or even a conference room for larger meetings to assist prevent the afternoon slump. Each of these tactics provides consumers with more value than your product portfolio alone does.

9. A high value item may create a sense of urgency.

Occasionally, providing value can make your customers feel pressed for time. When this happens, make an effort to keep customers interested in methods that retain high customer value.

Customers are accustomed to the value they receive, especially from well-established companies. Customers in your industry understand that demand will rise when value is raised to new heights.

Customers occasionally experience this sense of urgency merely when things are on sale for the lowest prices ever, as is the case with "Black Friday" deals.

In some circumstances, regional goods might be temporarily offered in another locality. A comparable sense of urgency is generated by this window of restricted access.

2.3 BUILDING REPUTATION

Establish a good reputation

When it comes to generating positive customer value, your company's reputation can be quite important. When consumers have positive perceptions of your company or brand, they may choose your products or services even when rivals are offering lower rates, quicker shipping, or more discounts.

Building client value in many of today's markets requires more than just a good product or service portfolio. Customers want to be able to rely on businesses that share their values and long-term objectives, brands they trust.

Make sure you constantly provide high-quality goods or services if you want to start developing a great reputation. If you can continually promote a superior customer experience, customers who previously made a purchase from you might do so again.

After creating a service catalog you are proud of, think about the hobbies and tastes of your potential clients. You may quickly boost your standing in the eyes of your customers if you can take action to openly support causes they care about.

Your reputation can have a significant impact on the status of your overall consumer value, often even more so than the goods or services you provide.

- **You will be noticed by prospective investors.** If you are trying to stand out in a crowded market while offering in-demand goods or services, it could be difficult. If your company is actively looking for investors, existing competition may prove to be a significant hurdle.

You have an opportunity to stand out when your business introduces new items, adopts new policies, or otherwise modifies its business model to draw clients in a crowded market.

You put yourself in a good position to attract investors when you exhibit innovation, the capacity to continuously adapt to changes in your market. Investors in a crowded market do not always favor businesses with the highest sales; instead, they choose businesses that are aware of market change and flexible enough to adapt.

Do not be hesitant to adopt innovation as a firm. Potential investors will see that your company is a wise investment prospect if you are willing to change with your market.

- **You increase opportunities for involvement** Value is frequently powerfully communicated throughout the sales stage in various marketplaces. Customers frequently seek further information from salespeople when they are considering a good or service. Enhancing customer value is a great opportunity during this engagement stage. A salesman who goes above and beyond to educate a potential customer can significantly raise the perceived worth of the product in the eyes of the client.

CHAPTER 3

3.1   ENHANCING YOUR OFFER

There different ways by which you can enhance your offer:

3.1.1 Scarcity

Scarcity marketing has a bad reputation in e-commerce. It could seem like a false or deceptive sales gimmick. However, the scarcity principle still applies: People give more value to things they believe to be scarce and less value to things they believe to be abundant.

For instance, Yeezy sneakers are more expensive than Nike shoes since they aren't always in stock. The business instead makes limited quantities of new products available. It is believed that just tens of thousands of pairs of shoes are available for purchase in some of these collections.

Utilizing scarcity marketing allows you to capitalize on your customers' fear of losing out. Its foundation is the psychological axiom that people crave things they are unable to have. Brands using product scarcity techniques would limit the quantity or window of time during which customers might buy a product in order to increase perceived value and sales.

Scarcity marketing examples:

- Flash sales
- Countdown timers
- Limited-time offers
- Limited stock
- Limited quantities and product drops
- Social proof

- Urgency in copy
- Cart reservation

Flash sales

Flash sales are last-minute announcements of sales that last only a short while. They can be a terrific approach to create urgency because they get clients fired up and prepared to buy right now.

Customers will pay far more attention to your firm's marketing materials and announcements if your company becomes recognized for its flash deals.

Flash sales are advantageous due to:

- A flash sale can be advertised via a variety of channels: Ads, social media, email marketing, and SMS
- They provide an excellent chance to thank current clients by letting them know first.
- If you require cash flow, they can supply a rise in sales.

You might have taken advantage of Bose's flash sale on the QuietComfort 45 if you were subscribed to its email list. The company advertises a one-day flash sale in this email that saves customers $50 on the QuietComfort noise-canceling headphones, which normally cost $329.

2. Countdown timers

On your product page, include a countdown timer in addition to the sale's end date. A visual timer has more effect than an end date. The client is actually counting down the remaining time.

Customers are convinced to act right away by the sense of urgency created by countdown timers. You've probably encountered countdown timers in e-commerce stores before.

You may utilize countdown timers in a few different places, one of which is directly above the Add to Cart button on your product page. Check out the countdown timer used by medical equipment shop Medici equipment Co. to advertise its storewide discount.

3. Limited-time offers

A promotion deal with a restricted window of time is known as a limited-time offer. It gives a specific deadline for when the promotion will stop and become unavailable. The scarcity principle states that when a product is harder to obtain, it increases in value in the eyes of the consumer.

Limited-time deals may appear as:

- Sales
- Discounted prices
- Free gifts
- Exclusive products

- Free shipping

Examples of limited-time deals are most prevalent on Black Friday Cyber Monday (BFCM). Brands take advantage of the holiday shopping rush by holding a one-day event when everything is sold at incredibly low prices.

For a variety of reasons, brands also launch time-limited promotions throughout the year. For instance, Kyle Cosmetics recently held a summer sale that included both a discount and a free gift. Customers received a complimentary jelly pouch and 25% off any purchases over $40.

On its homepage, Kylie Cosmetics also provided precise information about the campaign. You can find the exact time the offer expires (July 4 at

11:59 p.m. PST) beneath the headline sales pitch.

4. Limited stock

The number of things still in stock is displayed as a further scarcity marketing strategy. The simplest method to achieve this is to simply highlight the quantity you have left and display the number of items you currently have in stock on the product page itself.

This strategy has undoubtedly been used before on an Amazon product page. How many things are still in stock is indicated by Amazon in the right-hand column beneath the price.

5. Limited quantities and product drops

Telling clients how many you have to sell rather than letting them know how many are still available is another technique to create scarcity with restricted supplies. When you only produce and sell a certain amount of a product, such as a limited edition or limited run, employing this technique typically yields the best results.

Drops are not just for major influencers and international businesses. Clothing company Donni, famed for its stylish basics, also had success with product drops during the pandemic. Alyssa Wasko, the company's founder, started launching individual styles without warning in an effort to cheer up customers who were going through a difficult period. Glossy is informed by her that the consumer response was "insane" and that the product would "sell out in minutes."

6. Social proof

According to the psychology principle of "social proof," we base our decisions on the beliefs and conduct of others. It confirms a customer's decision and indicates that a product is worthwhile. Actually, 40% of consumers claim to trust online evaluations just as much as personal recommendations from friends and family.

Additionally, social proof demonstrates your authority and popularity to online customers, which might arouse sentiments of passivity and encourage transactions. For instance, ModCloth uses star ratings on their product sites to foster confidence and boost conversions. Additionally, customers can browse internet reviews to learn from others' purchase experiences and determine whether the item lives up to their expectations.

More sales can be generated by using social proof along with additional scarcity and urgency techniques like stock limits and countdown clocks than by using a simple product page. Use a tool like Judge.me to gather consumer reviews (along with images and videos) and display them on your website.

7. Urgency in copy:

To generate scarcity, you do not just need to display the quantity or sell a small number of a product. Urgency can also be greatly increased by the copywriting you employ on your website, marketing materials, and emails.

Note the language Mizzen+Main uses to describe its new shirts. Mizzen+Main makes me want to visit their store right away by warning me that "They are going quick!" rather than just saying, "Hey, new shirts are in our store, check them out!"

8. Cart reservation

Online merchants lose $18 billion each year due to shopping cart abandonment. Reserving shopping carts for individuals who leave them behind is another example of a scarcity marketing strategy. This procedure prevents other customers from purchasing the items by keeping them in the shopping basket for a while. You then let the customer know what is left.

If you know the customer's mobile number, you may quickly follow up through text message and include a link to the abandoned cart. Observe how SuperCoffee notifies the recipient that their basket is about to expire with a hilarious, slightly snarky text.

The link can be clicked by the recipient to take them to the shopping cart when they are ready to finish their purchase. Purchases of their previously added items are now possible.

Additionally, if you know the customer's email address, you can contact them there. In the example below, Luno, a company that sells automobile camping equipment, makes a succinct statement. With a graphic and a call to action that point the customer to their shopping cart for a purchase, the email informs them that Luno has saved the cart for 24 hours.

When making a limited-time offer, keep the sale period realistic. Offering bargains for one hour is not a good idea. If the window is too small, people may reject the bargain. Researchers from the University of East Anglia discovered that when individuals had more time to ponder an offer, they were more likely to accept it.

The likelihood for consumers who were found to be low procrastinators was still 26%. You can reduce the likelihood that your clients will put off making a purchase by generating a product or time shortage. While you do not want to convert all of your website visitors into passionate buyers, you do want to motivate them to take action right away, and that is where the concept of scarcity comes in.

By inventing a product or time shortage, you can add apparent scarcity to your store.

How scarcity marketing works

The worry of consumers about missing out can be quite influential. There is a potential that website users will delay and try to delay completing a purchase. According to a study by the Centre De Recherche DMSP, consumers who were deemed to be strong procrastinators had a 73% risk of delaying making a purchase decision.

Consumers who were discovered to be low procrastinators still had a 26% risk of being so.

By creating a product or time shortage, you can lower the possibility that your customers would put off making a purchase.

While you don't want to convert all of your website visitors into passionate buyers, you do want to motivate them to take action right away, and that's where the concept of scarcity comes in. By inventing a product or time shortage, you can add apparent scarcity to your store.

Make responsible use of the scarcity concept.

It's important to remember that enormous power also comes with great responsibility. Scarcity can be very effective if the product and consumer are the appropriate fit. The best approach to this activity is not to deceive people or create a false sense of scarcity.

Marketing that uses created scarcity in an overt way can alienate consumers and damage your brand.

Keep the following ideas in mind:

- You must base the scarcity you create on something. Why do you only have such shirts available for a short while? What makes this product a limited edition? Simply adding a countdown timer to a product page won't increase sales. The countdown timer needs to display a sale or an offer that is about to expire (like next-day shipping).

- Lackluster sales are not always remedied by scarcity. For something to be truly helpful, there must initially be some demand for your products. Similar to when Apple releases a new phone or tablet, there is already a demand for its goods. The demand for and desirability of Apple products are only increased by their initial scarcity.

- Don't go overboard. You don't want to appear to be putting pressure on your clients. The main goal of perceived scarcity in your company should be to motivate decision-makers rather than compel consumers to purchase items they do not want. When done incorrectly, producing scarcity has the side effect of causing buyer's remorse.

- If clients feel forced into making a purchase, they may regret it, request a refund, and think badly of your company.

Use scarcity strategies in your digital marketing plan to increase sales.

In addition to discounts, using urgency and scarcity to drive sales is a great strategy. They excite customers, which motivates them to act quickly before the opportunity disappears.

If scarcity makes sense for your store, think about modifying one example to your business. Even a small change, such as how you phrase the quantity of a product still available, can have a major impact on conversion rates.

The red writing and thoughtful positioning make sure that customers won't miss the message. It serves as a reminder that the time for the discount is running out as the seconds pass.

Not all countdown timers must stand out by being red. A soft green countdown bar is used by the women's apparel company ModCloth to advertise a brief sale. Customers are informed about the 40% sale on a few items by the bar that remains at the top of the product page.

3.2 HOW TO MAKE YOUR SALES PRESENTATION MORE URGENT

You might include a countdown timer or a due date in your offer to instill a sense of urgency in your sales presentation. The fact that your product is only on sale for a short while or that your first 10 new subscribers will get a special bonus or discount are things you might highlight. Use phrases like "don't miss this chance," "act now," or "this is your last chance" to emphasize the urgency of your offer. However, make sure to stick to your schedule and that it is realistic and attainable. Otherwise, you run the danger of losing the prospects' trust in and respect for you.

How to create urgency

1. Be aware of your customers' problems

If you do not know who you are selling to, you will never be able to close any deals. How were you able to? You will not understand what motivates your intended audience. As a result, you will not be able to predict which value propositions would favorably affect your prospects' decision-making processes.

How does this apply to the urgency of sales? You can offer your company's products or services as a workable solution when you are aware of your customers and their particular problems. Since prospects want to find a quick solution to their problems, this suggestion will inevitably create urgency.

6. Aid potential customers in understanding the price of tardiness

Consider this: You have been communicating with a specific prospect for some time. You have called them several times and left a dozen follow-up messages for them. They have spent many hours researching your particular offerings on the website of your business.

The sales procedure is going as planned, and you can already tell that the purchase will be completed soon. Just make sure your potential customer never loses sight of their problem.

Sales representatives frequently forget why their prospects need their products because they are so enthused about a prospective sale. They become distracted by case studies and features, neither of which are crucial to the prospect's purchase decision. Stop allowing this to happen to you! Instead, make sure that your potential customers are constantly aware of their problem, the benefits of solving it, and the reasons why your products are the best answer.

Asking them the correct questions at each stage of the sales process will help you achieve this:

What part of this issue frustrates you the most?

When would the ideal moment to address this issue be?

What are the unintended consequences of delaying action on this issue?

How does this issue effect [insert the measure that matters to your prospect]?

How many employees in your company are impacted by this issue?

How would you personally be affected if this issue was resolved?

How can you convince your supervisor that this issue is important enough to address?

What statistic would most accurately depict your new success if this issue was resolved?

3.3   BONUSES

How to Make More People Become Customers by Using Bonuses in your Business:

Using "bonuses" when selling a good or service can help you attract more clients who will pay for your goods or services. How do bonuses work? You give someone who buys one of your premium offerings a little something more (for free!). (However, you already knew that. There are correct and incorrect methods to approach your bonus offerings, as you can probably anticipate, and we will discuss these today. But let me first share with you a few other things I have observed other individuals doing.

Bonuses are helpful, but not when you use them excessively and become exhausted. People are beginning to favor courses that can impart the best knowledge in the shortest amount of time. Create a 10-minute video instead of a 30-minute one if you can get your point across more effectively. Similarly, do not develop 18 distinct incentives simply because you believe it "sounds better" if you just offer two bonuses that are exactly what you know your audience wants or needs.

The bonus brainstorming formula

Your bonus should not be about "how to take better photos with an iPhone" if your product is about "how to file your taxes as a freelancer." Obviously, I suppose. However, a lot of people give away bonuses that have nothing to do with their core product because they believe that doing so will make their program seem more valuable. Whatever your extras are, they should enhance your core proposition.

For the aforementioned example, a better "bonus" may read, "A 5-page guide to help you decide whether to turn your business into an LLC or remain a sole proprietor." This bonus works because it comes before you file your freelancer taxes, which is why.

Ideally, they should select one of the following two options after taking into account your bonuses:

Precursor: Give someone the information they require to feel prepared to utilize your paid product, or persuade them that using it is possible.

As a post-cursor, provide them with resources they can utilize to put what they have learned into practice after acquiring your paid product.

Assign your bonuses a reasonable dollar amount.

It will be helpful if you genuinely disclose the amount of your bonuses. You might just tell them they are getting a free e-book as a bonus, but the price of an e-book can range from $5 to $75, depending on the book's content. What is the value of your bonus given what it contains?

Naturally, if your bonus is a product you already offer, choosing a monetary value is simple. To ensure that others understand its genuine worth, you might wish to assign it a fair monetary value if you created it particularly to be utilized as a bonus.

Don't distribute everything.

As we mentioned in the introduction, you DO want to give some extras, but offering 90 different goods for free can discourage buyers from purchasing your product or service. Do you recall the "I'm too busy" era we once experienced?

In general, 4-5 distinct bonuses work well. We will examine some specific scenarios in which you will want to apply bonuses in your business later on in this piece. Furthermore, as you shall see further down, building your perks need not be a time-consuming process. Your bonus may occasionally be a 5-page manual. Other times, a

Facebook group will be used. Consequently, there's no need to overburden yourself or your potential clients.

What is a bonus that you can use?

What makes them so fun is the diversity of bonuses. I advocate the following bonus categories and have seen them:

Bonuses That Are Community-Oriented

page on Facebook

Slack team Forum entry for an event or retreat nearby

Bonuses That Put Value First webinar recordings

E-book e-guide, which is essentially a shortened e-book

Workbooks or worksheets

live workshop recording for an online course

a daily schedule or calendar that lists their obligations and due dates

Bonuses That Are Time-Focused

Q&A sessions or individual coaching sessions with you

Depending on how the product fits in, some sort of "audit" or "review" of the customer's website, exercise routine, attire, etc.

interviews in real time with accomplished people in your niche

These are just a few examples of the kinds of things you may add to your course as bonuses. Naturally, not all of them ought to be incorporated. Also bear in mind that you don't always have to create something new for your product in order to use it as a bonus. Hello, what? How does that work exactly?

Then, rather than coming up with a ton of new products, you might already be putting a lot of extras into the primary product itself. Those can be regarded as extras. If your offering is an e-course that contains both, reposition the Q&A calls and Facebook group as "bonuses" rather than elements that are essentially included in the course.

It takes the same amount of work to produce, but the gap between your finished product and the "frills" you add to it is getting wider.

If you are creating an e-course or workshop, another piece of advise is to include a "community" bonus to the mix when deciding which bonuses to choose. Creating some sort of community where your students can hang out is a great way for them to engage, discuss ideas, and for you to give your clients individualized coaching.

Now that you have some ideas for bonuses, where can you use them to help your business expand?

Bonus for Quick Action Webinars

When you hold live webinars, adding a "Fast Action Bonus" can significantly boost your revenue. It is what? You only give this bonus to customers who make purchases during the live webinar. Therefore, when making your pitch during a webinar, be sure to mention that this specific incentive is only available to those who buy before the webinar closes. Fast Action Bonuses can have a significant impact on your webinar sales since they make people feel more pressure to buy now.

How many items have you considered purchasing and then decided against? And I don't only refer to digital goods or e-courses! But if those things included a "Fast Action Bonus," it would be much easier for you to determine whether you truly want the item, for better or worse.

Start-Up Bonuses Bonuses should always be offered when launching anything (a product, a service, even a Kickstarter campaign!), since they increase the value of the initial offering and serve as an additional incentive for people to sign up.

You might wish to space out your benefits or add a few extras on top of the first bonuses throughout your launch in order to boost sales. Start, for instance, with a couple of benefits that all clients will receive. Then, give an extra reward to those who sign up during the first 48 hours. To give customers a fresh incentive to join up, you may also consider adding a brand-new bonus in the midst of your launch (when sales are often at their lowest). If your incentive adheres to the "bonus brainstorming formula" we previously discussed, it should undoubtedly increase the number of people who say "yes" to your program and make them believe that it is feasible.

Package Rewards

manage a service-based company? You could also benefit from bonuses! To make your more expensive and comprehensive packages even more alluring to potential consumers, consider giving incentives. Your friends may be more likely to choose the larger package since they will also receive some sweet benefits in this way. I strongly advise employing the above-mentioned "launch bonuses" technique if you're launching a new service.

To boost sales.

There may still be times when you need money straight soon, despite our careful planning. For instance, you might discover that you won't have enough money to pay your rent this month due to a financial emergency or a sudden expense.

Consider conducting a "sale" of one of your goods or services if you find yourself in a tight spot. However, try offering a few time-limited benefits if they make a purchase within the next 48–72 hours instead of a discount (which could cause people to think your brand is "cheap"). The deadline emphasizes the need for customers to act quickly, and the additional benefits, which increase the value of your program, persuade them to buy.

3.4 GUARANTEES

Give a money-back assurance Gaining a customer's trust and getting them to purchase a company's goods or sign up for a subscription service can be accomplished by offering a money-back guarantee. A money-back guarantee policy can be developed by sales managers and company executives and may be applicable to specific goods and services. An organization that sells tutoring might, for instance, provide a money-back guarantee if, after three months of weekly tutoring sessions, the student's grades remain the same or decline.

4.4 NAMING CONVENTIONS FOR PRODUCTS

Having difficulties coming up with a name for your product? We have compiled a list of best practices to help you generate amazing ideas.

Specify a goal for it.

Keep in mind the company's mission and principles. When brainstorming, use these as a starting point; you should be able to come up with a number of ideas. Select a name that is associated with your brand identity to fit into your whole marketing strategy.

Less is more.

Shorter names are typically easier to remember. If your product name is brief, uncomplicated, and simple to spell, your customers will be able to remember it. Additionally, sharing it on social media will be made easy for them.

Make it stand out.

If you have a unique, memorable name, you will stand out from the competition. Depending on your market, competition could be a problem. A name that sticks out will be noticed by your customers, who will hopefully remember it.

Verify that it is easy to pronounce.

On paper, that certainly seems great, but have you ever tried saying it aloud? Remember that your customers must be able to talk about it, recommend it, and ask questions verbally.

Make sure it is noticeable.

To enter probable names, use Google Translate. This vital step ensures that even if your brand name was made up, it does not have an unexpected connotation in a different language. Although it sounds simple, the Spanish word "asquerosa" actually implies unpleasant, which is not what you want people to associate with your business.

Make certain it is visible.
Check to see if speaking and writing are easy.
As we just stated, your product name should be easy to say and spell. Once you have pronounced the name to family, friends, and coworkers, ask them to write it down or read it aloud.

If they falter and the outcomes indicate that there is a problem, it is time to search once more for a different name.
complies with your brand's or product category standards

What is the purpose of your business? What are you trying to accomplish? What values does your brand stand for? The answers to these questions have an impact on all of your brand's decisions, including the decision to name a product.

In certain firms, there are guidelines regarding item names. If this describes you, you must decide whether to choose a name that adheres to tradition or departs from it.